R.F. LANGLEY

COLLECTED POEMS

CARCANET

infernal methods

First published in 2000 by
Carcanet Press Limited
4th Floor, Conavon Court
12-16 Blackfriars Street
Manchester M3 5BQ

A CIP catalogue record for this book
is available from the British Library
ISBN 1 85754 448 X

The publisher acknowledges financial assistance
from the Arts Council of England

Set in 10pt Ehrhardt by Bryan Williamson, Frome
Printed and bound in England by SRP Ltd, Exeter

COLLECTED POEMS

Contents

For Barbara

Acknowledgements

Most of these poems have previously appeared in three collections
published by *infernal methods*: *Hem* (1978), *Sidelong* (1981) and *Twelve
Poems* (1994); and in *Jack* published by *Equipage* (1998). 'Man Jack' was
published as *Poetical Histories No 30* (1994), 'The Barber's Beard' and
'Tom Thumb' as an appendix to *Poetry in Favour of the World* by Peter
Riley, *Form Books Occasional paper No 6* (1997). Some have appeared in
A Vision Very Like Reality, Equofinality, Arts Report, The Gig, and *P.N.
Review*. Some also in *A Calendar of Modern Poetry: P.N. Review 100*
(1994) and *The Harvill Book of Twentieth-Century Poetry in English*
(1999). To all of whom thanks.

Mariana

And, looking out, she might
have said, 'We could have all
of this,' and would have meant
the serious ivy
on the thirteen trunks, the
ochre field behind, soothed
passage of the cars, slight
pressure of the sparrow's
chirps – just what the old glass
gently tested, bending,
she would have meant, and not
a dream ascending.

And, looking in, she might
have seen the altering
cream of unemphatic
light across the bevel
of the ceiling's beam, and,
shaken by the flare of
quiet wings around the
room as martins hovered
at the guttering, she
might have soon settled for
these things, without the need
for certainties elsewhere.

So, 'Please,' she would have said.
'We could,' she would have said,
and 'Maybe,' mildly. Then,
selling out, buying in,
the drawling light and the
quiet squall of martins'
wings again, again, she
might have soon discerned her
self, seeing them. Not things,
but seeing things. And with
such care, it would be like
being shown what was not there.

It was the old glass cooled
the colours and transposed
them in a different key. It
chastened most of what the
sparrow said, and made an
affilatura of
the tree. She would have known
the consolation that
it gave, and smiled to see
the unthought-of tricks she
needed, and the sort of
liar she was, or might soon be.

As things came in, and as
they spread and sprayed, she could
have tilted up her face
in the soft fuss they made,
'encouraging the cheat
with shivering lashes,
tremulo, fermo, wide
or tight, intending
to confuse her sight until,
perhaps, she dared to make
a try – to find her own
cupid in her own eye.

To such a scene, amongst
such possibilities –
the downright, matter of
fact determination
of ivy on the trees,
wriggling queerly under
the examination
of the glass, the steady
sunlit room, fluttered by
each martin as it made
its pass – to all of this
she might have deftly given

a lash, until there were
sequins in the air and
surreptitious cupids
glancing everywhere. They
pricked their wings. Their arrows
spun away with thinnest
silver chirruping. They
were miraculous, picked
by her to be beyond
belief – believing them –
the lie she told to throw
the truth into relief.

Into the pure relief
of ordinary light.
But now she must have all
of this, compelled to see
by possibility
just what the glass finds real
enough to bend, jolted
by tilting shadows that
the martins send, seized by
the amorini, who,
being unreal, demand
her head for what they steal.

The Upshot

We leave unachieved in the
summer dusk. There was no
need for you rather than me.
Here is the unalterable truth.
Outside the open door peculiar
bugbears adopt the dark, then Kate
passes across. Next to nothing
depends on her coming in.

Here are the eight absurd captains
whether they are seen or not. Here
their sixteen certain shadows on
the whitewashed wall. Here a hundred
ruffles, grey and jade, coolly laid.
My hands and feet are already lost
in this country, with the immediate
sadness which no one has to believe.

The captains have not moved though
earlier the peep of day had staked
everything on the ear and shoulder
of just one of them. But soon he was
smoothly snubbed like the other seven.
Now the individual is unimportant but
eight determined men stand penniless,
never a glance, in the silver evening.

The odd outside matter that twirled
around all day in the blebs of gold
needs thinking about. Gorgeous. Like
looking in a pool. My chickens drill
and strut, piping my own particulars.
I won't leave it empty. I save a cricket
on a hassock – anything that moves, lies,
quirks, shrugs, can make a face and wink.

The drollery of that fiery ear. A hunch
I held sparkling for some hours then
sacked with the real severity inherent
in the air of this place. My patent
excitement is poppycock which needed
volunteers. There's a chance Kate saw
more by not coming in, but I only peer
at the backs of the eight deaf heads.

In here we're less lit from the sky. We
count our twenty four and are in jeopardy.
It is my sleeve creaking or a faraway
kittiwake, baffled by woods, brushing
my ear with a jeweller's fingers – which
leave what? Next to nothing. So little
and so icy that the floor flattens in the
afterglow and a multitude stands up.

They stand up but don't go. All ready,
not started. Full stretch in their rigid
heads. Now, when I need it, I'm so close
to emptiness. But I know too much about
each of those eight fixed faces. Unless
you ask about the eyes. You do. Here's
the opening for the hundred tricks Kate
took by walking across, not looking in.

We leave unachieved in the
summer dusk. There are no
maps of moonlight. Things
stand further off. We find
peace in the room and don't
ask what won't be answered.
We don't know what we see, so
there is more here. More. Here.

The Ecstasy Inventories

We slow out and curve
then the deep lawlike
structures loom and bob
through. We sway up, shut
down and open, coolly, each
small hour. Quiet. Then
quieter still. When thin
rims of rose and powder-blue
start slightly and a marble
runs down a chute.

The beach is stocked with one cobble
and another until you have to be
particular. Which are these tiny kickshaws
or tricky grenades on the old mud peppered
for ten thousand years. I've been noticing
how they needed low light and stale eyes
to catch such humble cajolery, all along,
hatching with soft pops into articulate
habits or costumes or clothes in a great
press: the broad, the heavy, the paragon,
her most scarlet gowns.

A blackamoor spurs by. The picture
of an Moore on horseback. Who
next? In a wink, in a pinked
petticoat, in a waistcoat set
with spots like pinks, in one
worked with eyes, she ambles
the lanes. An Moore on
horseback. The picture
of an Moore on horseback.
St Jerome. Mr Coke's mother.
Worked with eyes. Blue eyes.

The warm sun in some June. This June.
Both Junes. Take now and make a then.
A room. A roomy workshop. Elderflowers.
Forget the scent. Here is a carpenter,
singing. It is a hymn. Never mind
the scent, forget the difficult
bushes. Here is the hymn
from this contented man,
who cuts a shield upon a mantelpiece,
good humoured and intelligent, but the
cool, slow-motion, vanilla, bombs, ribboning . . .

The cuffs, collar and bedclothes
have lace on them. The lace can be
mentioned as strips with discs
or wheels, as sunbursts
of logical straps, rays, pips,
split pods or crooked stars, as
much as counting and nice
as a pocketbook with every
species, in flight, at rest,
in colour. These inroads let
me understand, and mark
sharply. Over what? Over
brilliant quietness. The path
ends in the shadow of trees.
In the trees I can't see the tiny
passerines all about in the
sparkling confusion. Or
her cheeks. Or her chin.

Follow the come on to the regular
heart, where we shall read a long
page. O my friend! The thrilled
ripples and cicalas and the dark
where the path and the story
beat through! Boreas did love her,
here, illustriously, with cicalas
and rippling. I can hear some
Hippocentaur's lips take hold
of grass with the resilience of
grass and that old ripping sound.

Silver moon; thatch; owl on the gable
and twelve silver instruments on the desk
for surgery. Silver moon on the desk.
Twelve silver instruments constellate
behind clouds. Ready for the straw
bird in the house of feathers. Mild
fingers set twelve silver straws on
the shining wood. There is a soft
interjection, stroboscopic starlight
and the powers realign. In another
box there are two gold rings.

No virtuoso in the glade. Just
heaviness in the darkened boughs
and twigs akimbo say I must
leave my father, try to go, months
ago. Dancing Mickey tossed
his chin and both his arms so
that the yellow gloves shot
glittering out and curved
sadly away. Gone, in a rigmarole
of little evil grass. Come
to pass.

White hedonism cut on blue
intelligence and laced
with silver anxiety. Bravo.
It braces milady's cortical
layer to take what could
have been trauma but now snugs
a bee in a comfort. While ants
silkily fidget and moderate
men press on, juddering,
grinning, being temperate
because of the price of beer.

Folds pack away; there is no crash.
Amongst the carnivorous thus and
thus and thus come two grey eyes
as you think, 'Is it a comma's wings
make such a silky noise?' So the
grogram, the paragon, snarl. So
fighting for their ranges the
wolves forget the deer. Or they
would hunt them out. Peace.
Famine. In the border zones
the butterflies are all eyes.

In heaven, where they don't
refurnish often, there will
still be an old white bodice
cut on blue and two lost
roses. Sure, in Walpolelane
there is a whirlwind of old
clothes. You would have thought.
Until a closer look saw each
was not vexed but folded
in unexpected readiness
in the press of the storm.

Juan Fernandez

1

As we slowly exploit the opportunities
between the jug and the earth, sky, men
and divinities, somewhere along the hold
the spring has, the ring gaining the ear
as it is picked up, the print on the bar,
the head shakes, shakes in a rainbow nexus,
shakes to see the old marks so very plain,
shakes the traps in reflection, rattles
the concentration into scrapping across
the frame, fluttering, mercurial, rabbits
vanish, turning everything into a large
form protecting the small ones, a spread
hand mothering doubts, as, now that
whoever that was has stamped past, they
wrinkle out, filling the hollow again.
And now is the water as firm as a heel?
Back drops blue sky. Convenient steel.

2

Snug, close and whispering up a trade, we
peep abroad again to find the planets,
earth and stones still satisfyingly alike,
sanctioning a lot more familiar adventures,
though we absolutely don't explain that
impression. Toes. Tokens. Miracles. Don't
you fret. We are gently rocking again.
Which makes it wonderful to rediscover
the silky wet print and deliberately fit
the foot back in it. I stood like one
thunderstruck. It was too big. By a great
deal too big. It was not mine. Loose my
cattle. Demolish my bower and tent. Wear
very quiet clothes. I've left school and
nobody cares about my motives now. Nothing
is clearer and more simple than a row of
rabbits caught outright in common light.

3

It is a common experience to come upon a
pale, glittering house set far back across
a meadow. It is certainly inside you. Down
along hours of mumbling 'Hello', and for
the attention of nettles in their darkest
green listening uniform, whose steadiness
miracles your ridiculous modern feet. In
its nimble way the lease suggests you can
project yourself, be big as the ancestors,
in this tangy, tart-taking, distinguished
deal. 'It's a light touch,' he shouts back,
'that will cause a great burning!' To which
the response has to be a firm shake of the
head or a slight widening of the eyes. Then
he's hurrying up, laughing, with his silly
reassurance that 'It's only you!' and
another blue funk is absolutely everywhere.

4

The print over the bar is the order of release
and it's away home again, ransomed deep into
a second time, deep into a pale blue, silky
head, billowing, billowing, a mite of quick
silver rousing in the threads. It bites. The
smell of meths just opens slightly round the
lamps. The unexpected colours stare. The crowd
is wholly intent. A fluttering. A blaze. Then
justice on justice as prodigious striding
shadows come to shut under this foot that I
am putting carefully down. The self is felt,
as standing, fired, inside the diamond. He
elucidates every projection and teaches what
was hidden in the heart. Of what is really
here. Of nooks. Of ends. Of wrinkling leaves.
The sparrows to the trees outside. So quietly.
The leaves just open up and let them come.

5

And all along the breastworks the dominators lean
and sneer. And I sneak and look up and match snarl
with snarl. It has always been in me to know how
they snarl. And I've done it before as a child and
a dreamer. The power is in dark, steady beams. I
sneak and snarl. But now there's a tiny request. A
cautious sip which might be surprising. It is hair
brown, or even lavender. It is a faint roughness
that stops. A flickering that hops to a deep nest
where the old frame burst its black heart. And she
twinkles in there with a beakful of wriggling legs.
During the last stages of the struggle, like this,
and only through a medium of dim instruments, came
baby fact. A particularly gentle thrill. She wore
silvery bluegrey. Sparkling. Startling. And the
brooding self with all its vanity disappears. You
forget how it is. Then. Whizz. And a perfect catch.

6

Could be that, when the carpenter stops to look
up, just as he straightens, his first idea will
be to see what he's been chewing. And the late
afternoon will open into a stunning exhibition
of honey and pepper. The awkward handle of the
saw. Its shadow on the bench. The shadows of his
fingers next to it. Curling. The separate worm
holes in the wood. Nothing seems so alive as the
tense silence of this picture. A new assessment
has released everything into uninhabited islands.
Into a final order. No. No. No. Now style alone
replies tamarisk on the dunes. Curling. I am
indicated by a star. And a footnote. I have been
shot through. Some sort of dancer must have been
here. But command is taken now by those tiny
expert birds who perch, and glow, and whizz
and pick the pepper out of the closing air.

Matthew Glover

To start with throve heavy forest
this district, on its marl
thick blue marl

a wood, preformal

no stream showed downhill
no hill rose up
but like a seasurface
this tract waited
for a mark, for a —
they would call it

    navel

    which someone did
    and from which came
    great benefit: as they cut it
    out of the trees

    they had it
    first time here

        shape, clearcut
        opens the four directions
        cardinal points in the previous wrack
        hollywrack alder bramble oak old
        dragon

        in good shape now for
        them to go to bed
        point their feet south

            if they wish

and the roof
opens
the fifth way
that is, heaven

meanwhile, and because they
watched the moon, over the clearing
they had an image for growth and decay
implying resurrection.

the east edge of the parish now
is a stream in a sandy ditch;

a shelterbelt banks it:
alder, willow, some bigger trees,

and the scene here is,
at the hedge corner,

a fine, detailed bush, dead,
a wicker cage now

where three or more warblers
hawk at the flies.

and, as the light changes, they are soft
brown or soft yellow with such restraint

that their flanks
shew like ice

as they shift
the small fizz

of their flight
breaks into

your thoughts . . .

25

watching them is to see
the idea of a bird come

over into sight and sound,
momently, secretly, so

hard to see them in the air in
the bush there is no space

for implications: they have slender bills
and jet eyes; of colour

they have as much as the light gives,
not ever much beyond olive and white;

they keep themselves
within pure outlines.

In the midlands the village, everywhere
with its Open Field, system of which
little is known but
at its simplest two fields:
Westfield: Eastfield,
Northfield:
Southfield; each decade adding
towards the ultimate territorial limits but
all the time, sacred space, paradigm,
unfolding from the navel outward
to the line where villages will meet
or commons begin or
the colefield begin.

Enclosures in this parish cut up
the Open Fields round its centre
before 1758 and took the Commons

30 yrs later, fast, from the
declaration on the church door
to the Commissioners' meeting,
with maps and rules, at the 'Anchor',
15 days, one objector, one resident
undecided. From here we have,
minor changes only, the present fields,
squarish, five to ten acres, hedges
with quickthorn inset with elm,
spaced, bright willow by the waters.
Fox cover too, in odd corners, 'gorses',
Stonnall Gorse, Cock Heath Coppice, with
ruled borders; and the straighter roads
were laid now, 1800, by the 5th April:
wide verges where blackberry grows
and cow-parsley. Farmers moved out
into their new fields with red brick
Georgian or Victorian, fast as they could.
Here, though, is Mill Green: the stream
through the millpond, through the osier bed,
a small settlement at the boundary of parishes
because of the water. Here then
the lane is narrow, the older fields
wide water-meadows, the air rank, the
small crack willow.

the sharp fizz
of the wings

whose white lining
glints like signals

as they jump in
the basket of dark

brushwood, distracts,
like Matthew Glover,

resident, who would not
speak for or against.

      All is lost
      by such an arrangement

      took a walk in the fields and
      saw an old wood stile
      taken away

            all my life

      a favourite spot
      which it had occupied

      the posts were overgrown
      with ivy it seemed
      akin to nature and
      the spot where it stood
      seemed taken on lease
      for an undisturbed existence

      all my life

      my affections claim
      a friendship
      with such things
      the small willow

            the small crack
            willow is dull

            until the low
            wind creams it

up with a purr
like bunches of

paper it blows
it purrs it purrs

Owning very little land
rated at eightpence
very little soil

maybe I did wish
to oppose the Bill

but I dared not do it
for fear I had missed . . .

A long time
I imagined

each square
five acres

I turned it
over

in my mind

no distractions.

The shapes seemed abstract
but handled well

at all speeds

were, in a way
pure, that is

admirably active, ingenious and bold
and operating on variables to effect
whatever transformations are permitted
by their definition.

as fair, you may say, as
citing the cycles of the moon.

But how
it shone!

used to, with the radiance
of delightful allegories!

Allegories. Some things were
full of fame; it will be long

ere their memory, their tales of it,
it might be a stile, or a willow
where tracks met all my life . . .

the moon, the lining of
the leaves

of the wings

Here
the light going
few notice the corner bush
is already an airy cage
where small birds flip
almost silently.

No tales about the willow-wren
please! What? Noise?

noise?

      he is too slight, almost
for one word

      he is
a bird for this moment and
the next

but no more

and his colours
excite no feelings, almost
no hint

      or half a hint

not enough to decide.

Saxon Landings

1

Here is of all the very this
is at last to keep the signals
lit or soon, they might, who knows
for sure the shore to either
hand so quickly in the haze. And
this could, once, so it has been
solid and level, hold on, then
here is inside your head laid out
in zones of shells and leaves like
you always hoped, not real, but
cool, it throws white light in
your face would you step out
under trees under tumbling trees
hold it still in both hands.

2

Through by the door, in the fright
of it's done, it's shot in a
click, though it's not light yet
the smells are sharp the bricks
don't blink, you blind as you
tell it this is action action
action and the treasure, heavy
silver, warm lids, mother table,
olives and cheese and bread and
possessiveness of a simple love
the whole zoned, beaded and scrolled
just gloats, it just gloats and
push it somewhere away into soft
loam and leave it afloat there.

3

Once they believed it but since it
is diction, the pipes in the wood
or limber vine and the bland
country where Bacchus and Pan
defeat Hercules. They lift him.
The drunk. Hush. Lay him down in
the sound of his name on the ground
of our home these are loan words we
never except as ledges of leaves of
shells this is keepsake and darling
and silver in moonlight is cold
twice cold, it throws white light
on your face you look blood
less in the porch's daze.

4

Your calm, my lady, has been
to have it your own, and known
hot to your ankles your knee
on the seat and talking windows
looking windows into arcady,
delectable, putting out white
poplar forming with your berry
mouth leaves or winter acorns
where your mood took listening
to there shall it suffice your
poet to have sung but this is
a very it cannot, slung on my
hips out my corner eye, rake
hell, orgies, waters, unlimited fury.

5

Save yourself stop this reflective you
can't think it sling it and run my
voice is quite shrill because while
you've been ships have beached, some
bird yelped, the face of a god looks
straight at you were eating off his
sacrilegious like a picnic his eyes
pop fish squeeze out his hair he really
rages lady! your chair spins his flashes
darken the windows his mane his mouth
is an open road under tormented forest
trees you walk gasping down his roaring
maw carrying your silver dish still
carrying you've been given a silver dish.

Arbor Low

White
arse
birds nip off stones which face
down. The birds tight on hip
fop and haptoe. The stones

dead. Sigh. There. But birds
burn off the tips of the fallen with
particular
flicker off
continuous stiffs down countless

once. A deepening hiss. Zig
with, zig
like
colour ripped off a just
after you hush like you

look inside at the big
still stones in the parcel of
now. But
a rude
fig a smart right at

some who come carrying deep
sighs to bring off the big
glamp onto all that comes
bubbling
through shining

reams off
the dark
bodies that rise in pale
apprehension. The birds fig
off like bits that snap at

the wrapping, unwrapping of greedy
to pass back to wives, to friends,
with open bags the tons of immovable
to be
alone then

they drive off with just a small
faraway
in the
glove compartment and bubbles like
someone the champagne had an

amazingly vivid but
little but little
bright
farts
of the birds.

The Long History of Heresy

Under the roar walls ride their
warriors and that unstoppable
young lord without a sword who

was a murderer. In all that fury
he sees at once. And nods. As
if he heard a sound, turned round

and found a bird in the court. Dun
pavement through a rush of coloured
slippers. While down along the quiet

waits our man, old nose, star
tooter, under a tree, leaning on
a heavy kill he won't know how to

use. Its polished edge bristles
with a thousand rays, steely, rosy,
blurry, sticky with a mix of saps. So

much consideration. Some folded
leaves. Some pierced. Others eaten
to the veins. The flies, in silhouette,

moving about the memoirs. So deep
into the book. Improbable fiction.
Old smears. But in a trice the young

lord found it easy to forget. The glass
cracked and a shower of coloured seconds
sprinkled away. Suddenly our man brushes

meal off his neck. Light agitation and
grasshoppers mix into more and more
stars   stars   stars   stars   stars.

Sneak drops touch leaves. They
wink. Flicker. And flicker. I
rush round to throw cotton-reels,

pin-cushions, short silver chains
into each bush. To play 'Gone' with
all the toys. To fit bobs into many

many sorry mouths. Won't we soon know
the whole shape of the lady? Our man
can only groan and twirl the blade so

that the constellations sail out to
settle into different shadows. Fingers.
Moths. Daintiness. Hopes and memories

play lips and blinks with blues and
pinks. Sometimes the softness of a
shower seems so shrewd that the foliage

is an inferno. Too many pats to be
married. Tickled to bits. But then again
the encouraging warmth of tonight with

coloured lights in the pub garden, over
the green, steadily seen. This bench
is built round the trunk. You might see

them on moonlit bushes, on the twigs, on
the night war was declared. Their eyes
both bright and full. After an hour I

worked out that the establishment was due
to a grip I had on it all coming from this
astral crimpling at the root of my nose.

Always, close to us, are one or two
motionless, big leaves. Then the
labyrinth. Dim groups and crumbling

lights which we collect and feed. But
the young lord's determination is such
that only ghosts are waiting at the

next intersection, only fancies power
the cloudy foliage. He is to be going
through, and out, smooth, untricked,

hitting infinity in a spick of fire.
Anything might be his sword. Each time
he passes through he finds his friends

have more and more about them, but he
smiles. Didn't he kill one of them
once? What the patient intends to mean

is irrelevant. Anything, as it moves,
might now and then stop to nest and
rest, arranging some shade and some

interest. But such organisation is just
the stop itself, no more, a footprint,
here, moving some trash, pressing it

to stay. But only an indian would know
of such places, want to keep a prayer
where a ghost took a breather. Our man

remembers a few, and smiles, pressing
a clenched fist into his heart. Anything,
but anything, is the young lord's word.

He's one who never dreams of possession.
He speaks and brightly rustles up some
suggestions of this evening on the small

screen of trees, the commotion of flash
and asterisk, but he is not referring to
any of this. 'Listen,' he says. He says

'Straight, white water.' And listening
becomes glistening. Lightning contentment.
Which our man sees as taking place against

some storm, a silence in the heavens,
inside some sort of a travelling pause,
where a mature lady steadily feeds a

baby. 'Listen,' he says. 'The Naughty
Boilers.' And our man roars with horrified
excitement as he chases a furiously

damaged sparrow which he dares not quite
touch. Then, 'Dainty Dish,' he says, at
last. And the whole canopy begins to

patter under a spray of hot urine until
our man staggers in the pandemonium and
slop to fall flat, quite passive, crying

desperately, but quietly. How was I so
willingly defeated? I was forced to give
over when I felt the big drops piercing

the foliage overhead. The warmth of the
uncut grass. In impossible furrows. In
tufts. Near green. Dove gray. An unusual

rosy pink in the unmade hay. I can make
nothing of lover's violet and the dark
long throws. Of muffled rubies. Nothing.

Nothing. When you're taking my breath away.

Blithing

The first of the ecstasy
singers screams soft scissors
open fans of leaves and a prim
little crack trims millions
of tendrils off all round
the space

Now, careful. The fern
carpet itches with pieces
of charcoal and bargaining
chips but the little grey
cock hoods bid after bid
over his thousand-stick
orange blink orange blink
orange

it tastes wise
and very dry
this little
decided kiss
till out of
selected non
drip shadows
walk the raisins
and nuts

I should think I will probably
have to come here again. On
one of those wayside tabernacles
you could read 'Illumined the
placid sea' and 'Unequivocally

aware that we were seated on
the shore. Nov. 17th.' and on
we went under the spray which
trancelike bloomed

Why else the signs saying 'Deeper
In' and the huge unsplit banana
leaves and the thin edges
of listening, entire, swimming
through clear water with open
eyes after the neat pink prawns

O you, O you he
this, she this
here, once, and
again and again
fieldgate. Such
shadowing

Come, opus one, or
little loaf in
the shape of a
found in the rain
of fired bits after
the stupendous silent
explosion, one piece
in the shape of a
girl

Rough Silk

So it best be away from home.
Some travel. Somewhere sour.
So there is there. Shrewd
issue. Not yet mine. The

same in time. Low time and
over-rolled by cloud enormously.
And others small. White squip
alongside as we come. And having

come we found it what we'd said
but just the notes of dreams, put
away. So here. We made it
do. Near the coast. Night

air. Which we knew did not
much care. Nor did the poplars,
flexing, nor the bats,
bitterly. Nor the old, cold

tabletop. What we drank stood
ready to go like the side of
a head. We kept on drinking.
Unbidden thoughts come sometimes

lustrous. Maybe this.
This garden. Was about
to be run for us. Well
now. And poplars pursed.

Poplars supposed so, gave us
up, rolled open like a bodice
sighing. 'Poplars,' they said.
And we agreed. We

smacked that. In rows of
standard authors. Poplars.
We kept on drinking, risked
some bats and closed some

shrubs like scissors. No
need now, no need at all, for
more than our well-bound
popular readiness. Drunk

and relaxed, yes,
and tumbling his
hands spread his peace
ful fingers slowly

opening, bringing his
loosely heels over
his heads slowly
together, yes, to

a pressed and an
interlaced ten
finger moon and
so husky. Such creamy

trash our stinging moon comes
through. Some local gods pop
homemade gunnery so briskly
that fuel fires right across

the foliage and now there's
rippling red agreement and
ginger stabs crackle accurately.
Hellfire. The central tingling. All

women and ambush. Classification
goes wishing up the glass. Streamy
rules. In a golden dear. After
all. Creamy dusk. Boppin' Flossy's

tresses in the creamy, starry
dusk. Quippy to the sweetening
core. Oh Flossy. Persuasive
Flossy. Now you're here knees

flood and I don't need to row.
The shelves on the edges I
can reach, and they will be
limpid, even when the main

point rattles uncontrollably
stubborn and humbling. I am
voyaging already at unsmeared
horizons right and left, out

of earshot. Nobody stayed to face
that musky bosom flapping with
pipistrelle and fighting screams.
They all threw in together and

their trinklements simultaneously
scattered into white water. I
quietly remember that lost
property and I keep just one

cheap brooch, a shell, set
sidewise in pewter curls.

The Gorgoneion

Once more the menace of the small
hours and of coming to light and of
each sharper complication. There was
a loosening which let much neglected
detail out of the dark. You can't look
away once it's started to move. This.
Must. And so must this. In bitter little
frills and hitches. About in a suspicious
twiddle are the tips of someone's ten
fingers which could, sometime, touch
mine. Something it is I would. I know
the sort of thing. A sorry moth. Sheet
web on copper pipes. I catch my whisper
that I won't be coming back. This still
increasing presence is for the last time.
Then the beginning of an immense grip.

If this is a crisis then I'll tap away
at it. Reflections cringe and scamper,
hover, then come back to where it hurt.
They bunch into description and find
some manners to be taken with. But if
you're smart enough to stop the spider
you'll see his fingerwork is not quite
mine, although the threads jig less once
settled in Euclidean space. There is a
certain silky insidious amusement as the
sun runs off brilliant free copies both
in filigree and queerly inflected on the
wall behind. Stuck here like a simpleton
you begin to smile, to suppose, to think
in terms of proof, until you are hooked
by it. Until you are sucked as a thumb.

You'd think at least the small, quiet
things could be decided. But if you are
content enough, and happy to sit down,
then all at once you're riddled by the
fast trick of the demon doubling his
shadow on your knee. Once here, he posed
himself in complete seriousness with
just one quick rub of his hands. On
display to believers everywhere. Crimson
eyes fixed in a dealer's stare. Hold it
there. Nobody move. This odd arrangement
of the crumbs and the letters rigid on
the packets. Sugar. Blazing. The whole
deck. Slammed. The anger of what can't
move itself at all. Every damned object
in this room is rapt. And boobytrapped.

There's someone here who says it's simple
as loving a muffin. Someone who pulls on
his conjuror's gloves and kids things softly
along. I can't say it's my way. He reaches
across the table in the glare and touches
one thing after another as if none of it
mattered. I can't say if I've still got
teeth or ears. That must have been one hell
of an explosion! But all I recall is a
patter of warm applause. I wasn't there
ready to be born, and I didn't stand up
at the end, shrugging. I have to keep on
trying again, cracking my knuckles, snapping
my fingers, hoping to get them to feel
like mine. With hands like these I can
only be confident if I trump every time.

Hands shaking. Because none of this
will ever happen again. Old hands.
The backs of them. Professional
wrinkles. And still I don't know
their tricks. Nothing I want settles
anything. Put them down on the table
and let them rip. The wandering cards
twist and jumble through them. Light
from the streetlamp outside collects
some leaves and the lattice to assemble
them, briefly, here, on this wall where
all is forgotten as the mime at least
comes true, giving some sort of select
account of what things do. It's a strange
relief to transform your fretting into
the silent coiling of a phantom dragon.

Spellbound, now. By the slow movement of
the jewels settling into the heart of the hoard.
I doubt if I'll ever walk back to the village.
Sure cards come so smoothly that it's cruel.
Are there only things to endure? But the
cobwebs adjust to the sleepy lapse with
blue sputters or a flick of what might
once have been wings. A flash off the terror
of hopeless love. They started and glanced
at each other. The cavern is filled with
muttering. It is the witty little histories
of insects making some sort of sense of
mud, hair and dirt, until the thunder is
over, and warm rain begins to fall in this
stillness. Then a hand is laid down and
another turns itself upward to be clasped.

Man Jack

For Jane Williams & Bob Walker

So Jack's your man, Jack is your man in things.
And he must come along, and he must stay
close, be quick and right, your little cousin
Jack, a step ahead, deep in the hedge, on
edge, a kiss a rim, at pinch, in place, turn
face and tip a brim, each inch of him, the
folded leaf, the important straw. What for.
He's slippery and hot. He slides in blood.
Those lies he tells you, running alongside.
To and fro he ducks, and miserably
clicks and puckers up, and in his rage he
won't speak out, or only half. He's short. He's
dim. He'll clench his jaw. He's more than you can
take. He'll drop it all across the road and
spit and go. Over the years you'll have to
learn to pull him in and let him know. You'll
say, 'Today we'll have that, now, those other
apples. So. Oh, but you'll fetch them like I
seem to think I dreamed you did, and they'll be
like they always should have been, in action,
apples in the apples, apples' apples,
through and through.' And then you'll see what he can
do. He'll fetch them in and put them roughly
in a row. The scent will almost be a presence
in the room. 'Oh, but it hurt,' he'll say, 'to
pick across the stones, the different stones.
So many different pains.' Oh Jack. You
hick. You grig. You hob. You Tom, and what not,

with your moans! Your bones are rubber. Get back
out and do it all again. For all the
world an ape! For all the world Tom poke, Tom
tickle and Tom joke! Go back and carry
logs into the hall. And wait with lifted
finger till the eave drops fall. Your task. The
jewel discovered by the monkey in
the shine. Fetch that, and make it much, and mine.
Sometimes it's best if I forget to ask.
An errand boy with nothing up his sleeve,
who stops to listen to the rigmarole
to find he cannot leave without he's bought
the dog. Time out of mind. Just bring
what you can find. Apples. Twigs. Icicles.
Pigs. The owl that watches as we try a
phonecall from the isolated box. Jane's
disembodied voice. The owl that hears her
words. The moon that thinks about her baby.
Jack in the moon. Jane in Jill. The baby
coming sure and soon and bright and staring
at the apples which keep still. The owl had
no idea. More knew Tom fool. The apples
shine in everybody's eyes. Tom speaks
inside his cheeks. The moon talks from inside
his belly. The isolation sighs to think
of motherhood. We hear Jane's tiny words,
as does the owl, astonished, listening .
in the roadside wood. Jack gleeks inside
his only box of tricks for what has come.
All thumbs, he Tibs his Tom. It's apples and
it's owls. He bobs and chops and nips until
it's Jill engaged in paradise, with the

enchanted pips. Just in the nick with
only magic left. No use at all to
look at him as if he were a jug. As
if he were. A twig is evidently
a love bouquet. The apples are a gift.
The spellbound owl sits round as such
upon a shelf. Its silence cries out loud
as if you touched it on a wound. It is
embarrassed and delighted with what Jack
has found. And that it had, itself, the wit
required to secretly decipher it.
Until there is a sudden dip into
a silence in the silence, and the owl
has turned his head away and, frightened, stepped
off on his long legs into air, into
an emptiness, left by Jack who is not
there. He's gone too far. Though nothing drops, there's
nothing caught. The twig is two. The gleek is
three. There'd be a mournival in the four
but no one's counting any more. It stops.
The apple is not fire. And yellow is
not sweet. Jane's voice from miles away is just
a speck and almost lost, but yet it is
distinctly Jane, uninfluenced by the moon
she has not seen, the roadside where she has
not been, the owl who thought to pick a peck,
the apples she will never eat. The Jane
who cannot tell us yet the baby's name.
And, undeclared like that, it wins the game.

Jack's Pigeon

The coffee bowl called Part of Poland bursts
on the kitchen tiles like twenty thousand
souls. It means that much. By the betting shop,
Ophelia, the pigeon squab, thuds to
the gutter in convulsions, gaping for
forty thousand brothers. So much is such.
Jack leans on the wall. He says it's true or
not; decides that right on nine is time for
the blue bee to come to the senna bush,
what hope was ever for a bowl so round,
so complete, in an afternoon's best light,
and even where the pigeon went, after
she finished whispering goodnight. Meanwhile,
a screw or two of bloody paper towel
and one dead fledgling fallen from its nest
lie on Sweet Lady Street, and sharp white shards
of Arcopal, swept up with fluff and bits
of breadcrust, do for charitable prayers.
The bee came early. Must have done. It jumped
the gun. Jill and the children hadn't come.

How hard things are. Jack sips his vinegar
and sniffs the sour dregs in each bottle in
the skip. Some, as he dumps them, jump back with
a shout of 'Crack!' He tests wrapping paper
and finds crocodiles. The bird stretched up its
head and nodded, opening its beak. It
tried to speak. I hope it's dead. Bystanders
glanced, then neatly changed the name of every
street. Once this was Heaven's Hill, but now the
clever devils nudge each other on the
pavement by the betting shop. Jill hurried
the children off their feet. Jack stood and shook.
He thought it clenched and maybe moved itself
an inch. No more. Not much. He couldn't bring
himself to touch. And then he too had gone.
He's just another one who saw, the man
who stopped outside the door, then shrugged, and checked
his scratchcard, and moved on. Nothing about
the yellow senna flowers when we get home.
No Jack. No bee. We leave it well alone.

Jack built himself a house to hide in and
take stock. This is his property in France.
First, in the middle of the table at
midday, the bowl. Firm, he would say, as rock.
The perfect circle on the solid block.
Second, somewhere, there is an empty sack.
Third, a particular angry dormouse,
in the corner of a broken shutter,
waiting a chance to run, before the owl
can get her. The kick of the hind legs of
his cat, left on the top step of a prance.
The bark of other people's dogs, far off,
appropriately. Or a stranger's cough.
His cow's white eyelashes. Flies settled at
the roots of tails. What is it never fails?
Jack finds them, the young couple dressed in black,
and, sitting at the front, they both look up.
Her thin brown wrist twists her half open hand
to indicate the whole show overhead.
Rotating fingernails are painted red.

Who is the quiet guard with his elbow
braced against the pillar, thinking his thoughts
close to the stone? He is hard to make out
and easy for shadows to take away.
Half gone in *la nef lumineuse et rose*.
A scarlet cardinal, Jack rather hoped.
A tired cyclist in a vermilion
anorak. Could anyone ever know?
Sit down awhile. Jill reads the posy in
her ring and then she smiles. The farmer owns
old cockerels which peck dirt. But he is
standing where he feels the swallows' wings flirt
past him as they cut through the shed to reach
the sunlit yard, bringing a distant blue
into the comfortable gold. How much
can all this hold? To lie and eat. To kill
and worry. To toss and milk and kiss and
marry. To wake. To keep. To sow. Jack meets
me and we go to see what we must do.
The bird has turned round once, and now it's still.

There's no more to be done. No more to be done.
And what there was, was what we didn't do.
It needed two of us to move as one,
to shake hands with a hand that's shaking, if
tint were to be tant, and breaking making.
Now, on the terrace, huddled in my chair,
we start to mend a bird that isn't there,
fanning out feathers that had never grown
with clever fingers that are not our own;
stroking the lilac into the dove grey,
hearing the croodle that she couldn't say.
Night wind gives a cool hoot in the neck of
Jack's beer bottle, open on the table.
Triggered by this, the dormouse shoots along
the sill, illuminated well enough
for us to see her safely drop down through
the wriggling of the walnut tree to find
some parings of the fruit we ate today,
set out on the white concrete, under the
full presentation of the Milky Way.

The Barber's Beard

By Wednesday afternoon the wind has dropped
and there can be a shakedown. When I tap
the stems, black seeds jump off onto the snow
and fix themselves, so Jack says, according
to the disposition of the stars. It's
Alexander's dust, he says. It smells of
myrrh. It's Macedonian parsley and
also, he says, the surface of fresh snow
is more like fur. Each seed is caught in this
soft stillness as a small orb in its place,
tilting its face, and very tenderly
presented to the air. Now we expect
some music in the distance, from a house
which once was there.

                   Yes, Crustyfoot, we guess,
has made it to Piepowder Fair, and so
we know that Scipio will soon be back
from Africa. He'll blow in from the north
on Scandinavian gales. He'll be disguised
as a big thrush, dancing and flapping in
the cold bathroom and shouting out, 'I'm home!
I'm home!' Home in the roofless ruin up
the track, where Jack's map says 'Old Hall' and all
the drifts are deep and new. So, in the glow,
thorn by thorn, another diagram of
the strategy of last year's brambles has
been drawn.

I stop and stand where paths cross on
a Wednesday afternoon. Where else am I?
Somewhere there is a story being told.
I recognise Jack's voice that's quietly
telling it, as he describes how a man
is standing underneath a tree. How he
can see the standing of the man. He says
he feels his coat is comfortable and that
his shoes are doing well. The comfort of
his coat and what is watertight. He sees
that the ash is carrying its bunches
of ripe keys. The tree's carrying, and the
carrying of the keys.

                       The amazement
of Scipio in his shaving mirror.
Show me his shivering. Show me his quick
smile that flutters out about the edges,
and spreads as wide as the blue backs of what
must be a flock of fieldfares, suddenly
flashing round the lime-green branches of bright
winter hedges, and he . . . who ? . . we . . . at once
smell soap, and unexpectedly catch sight
of an awkward little grin attempting
to take flight, avoiding the circle of
reflected light. The only witness's
white face, frozen as he realises
that it's up to him. The him it's up to,
disabled by his role in last night's dream
and terrified that I am Hannibal.

Dustyfoot arrested in a blaze of
alibis, blinking like an idiot
and hinting he's a friend of Jupiter.

Are you all right? Is he all right? Here is
the list of all the dead elms in the ditch.
If you need to check the details you will
find the same old worn-out wormholes under
any scab of bark, and nothing about
the arrangements to tell you which is which.

Well then. Good morning Jack. Don't slip away.
Just for a moment there I thought you'd gone
while I was shaving you. Please look on me
as if I were your barber, concealing
my irritation that you're late today
by gossiping along in this sing-song,
hiding the gist of what I have to say
in brisker chatter.

          Suppose the felties
were to pick out every berry, laughing
mysteriously, 'Tchak, tchak!' That Jack himself
were the piper, and his son stole sweets. Which
silly little theft, for all the shouting,
turned out to be, not just a merry lark,
but princely, attended in the dark by
cherubim. Believe it. That the bodies
of the elephants rolled over on the
bitter snow. That schedules barked. That a freak
tide exposed the northern wall as they stormed
across the lagoon at Cartagena.

Then it would seem that all the answers could
be ticked. As if the nouns, detected in
the depths, began to glimmer deeper yet
beneath the things, so all the secret eggs
grew wings and even Hercules was sure
his debts would settle out of court at last.
Then keys could hang fast, waiting for a touch
in March from sleepy moonlight. Scuttling verbs
could trap elusive opportunities
among unlikely roots.

                                   But just as it
occurred to Jack that he might count the flock,
bird after bird displayed an ash-gray rump.
They've turned away and opened up.

                                               They are
about to go.

                              This is the moment when,
flummoxed to know what else is left to do,
Jack and the poet and the pronouns shrug,
take a breath each, and melt into the blue.

Tom Thumb

We should accept the obvious facts of physics.
The world is made entirely of particles in
fields of force. Of course. Tell it to Jack. Except it
doesn't seem to be enough tonight. Not because
he's had his supper and the upper regions are
cerulean, as they have been each evening
since the rain. Nor just because it's nine pm and
this is when, each evening since we came, the fifty
swifts, as passionately excited as any
particles in a forcefield, are about to end
their vesper flight by escalating with thin shrieks
to such a height that my poor sight won't see them go.
Though I imagine instantly what it might be
to separate and, sleeping, drift so far beyond
discovery that any flicker which is left
signs with a scribble underneath the galaxy.

My job, preparing for the dinner, was to peel
the shrimps. Decapitate them first, then, stripping off
the legs, pinch out, if they were females, all their black
and yellow eggs. And Jack, as usual, was not
at hand to help me do the damage, manage not
to curse out loud. We both know why. Distracted by
a resonating croak, he watched a heron stroke
unhurried to the south-east, past a rosy cloud
to the full moon. And then involved himself in how
the gnats above the chimney shared their worrying

together, working out their troubles in a crowd.
They must have done that every summer, all my life.
Jack says he never saw them doing it till now.
He makes a few impromptu jumping movements on
the lawn – his imitation of agitation
in swarms of innocent shrimps and prawns. And slow blood
slithers through my listening. This is the whine that
my poor ear can never hear, from the gnats high up
above the cowl. It's Jack's droll warning. Always there's
someone mourning. Always an invisible owl,
one of whose party tricks is knowing how to scowl.

Look Jack. I'm well aware what's going on when your
forefinger and your thumb reach out like that to give
the air a tweak, a twist, to tune in to the sound
you say I missed. What then? So maybe I pick up
a hum. Some fiddling from a belated fly that
landed unobtrusively on a hidden stem.
It's there. A minute elbow jiggling. Nothing more.
Doubtless this is the very moment when it saw
that you had marked *appassionato* in your score.

Between the nails of my forefinger and my thumb
I nipped the heads, pulled off the bushy whiskers and
bright pips of eyes. The shocked expressions came away.
But these were not actors. They were not wearing masks.
There was no second face beneath to recognise.
Jack didn't breathe. The midges seethed, where, I dare say,

there was an updraught through the flue, a warm one, though
without a fire. But he was staring higher at
the final suggestions of the swifts, rapidly
dashed off, carelessly punctuated with a run
of dots that flared, then melted immediately
into thin air. No doubt the lightning sketches of
the many different shapes of what he called despair.

Look Jack, again. Suppose that here we are in this
familiar room, and reaching out to shake hands
with our old shadow on the shiny knob of our
well-polished wardrobe door, to take out, once again,
the peculiar man we used to be before.
Can you pretend you need to have a photograph
of him in mind, to check we get exactly what
we think we'll find? Hello to last year's summer shirt.
The sleeves. Their flap and dangle. Halloo, halloo to
the ferocious gestures of the swifts, the flash and
chop, the quick contortion to escape at a new
angle, into a new glide. And every one I
know, because each is at once beyond compare. Each
action and its brilliant illustration simply
coincide. This is the fly, so tightly fitted
in its place I feel its savage elbows piston
in and out, though all it does is carefully wash
its face. I remember how, back in the bedroom,
I had to struggle with the shirt. But who buttoned
it so neatly? Then, in the garden, who reached out
so sweetly through the stinging nettles to disturb
the stem? Who delicately shook it so he could
identify the fly? What virtuoso played
that quiet capriccio? It was not Jack, nor I.

This thick-wit is my thumb. I cannot miss him for
he fetches wood, digs pignuts and ties shoe laces.
Three hundred motor units in him act as one.
He snaps open carapaces, pulls out white meat
and pinches off the faces. Sometimes he softens
the spiccato, smooths the document, signs my name.
Spirits obey. How goes the day? Oh, easily,
so long as you don't ask the way. I promised to
be here for dinner, come what may. For goodness' sake
you Jack, be dumb. Inevitable detail on
the moon, grows to perfection in a silent bed.
The heron spoke, and meant precisely what it said.
Gnats twinkle, and Jack glances down another list
of items due to be removed from the display.
Swifts vanish in full flight, against the changing of
the decorations from pale lemon to pearl gray.

Stop taking stock, and listen. They have briefly left
their voices, sharpened to incisive single points.
The screams of fifty little demons on a spree,
going home excitedly. Meanwhile, of course, the
heavens mutter, and the shopkeeper has put up
his safety shutter. Fireworks crackle for the end
of festival. Jack is jumping. The rhythm of
the gnats is hot. Up there, the chimney pot is squat.
We have finished eating supper. Stare at the cowl,
if you're so certain that the hunch must be an owl.

Poor Moth

Reasons run out and we are
ready to play backgammon
once again. Come on, I say.
I know when I am being
watched. Even in the washroom
here's a window left unlatched
and various small monsters
have nipped softly in to take
up key positions amongst
sunny patches on the walls.
Look at the little angels.
Chits of demons. Fools and spies.
Look at the conclusive way
in which their detail lies. One
touch would be catastrophe
or a whisper to the wise.
This mop is in the corner,
the hand towel folded to this
size. So everything is trim
in its replies. And three small
moths have six small eyes. Oh to
be merry with my friends! Oh
to be playing with only
matchsticks for the prize! Maybe
a lion would bleat, were it to
have goat's feet. Jack looks up a
chimaera in the book. He
flips casually through to
find it under 'J'. But it's
cross-referenced to where we
are today. To the sun stripes
on the green gloss paint, the types
of grass moth, who they're working
for, and why they put this mop

behind this door. The problem
in its purest form. There's Jack.
A figure I imagine
I can see far off in a
dark library. He's deep in
the reference section, where
a distant desk lamp bends his
shadow round the corner of
the stack. The librarian
has forgotten him. His arm
is lifted to the shelf. He's
fingering the spine of an
encyclopaedia which
he's just put back. It told him
something terrible about
himself. The revelation
prickled, and his fear struck me
as I was turning off this
tap. The echoes slip into
a quiet gap. I notice
I am breathing. Carefully.
I have to understand how
it was settled that the moths
came here. Signed up and waiting
with their wings wrapped tight. And ticked
twice. A double tick to make
it clear they have been checked and
are correct. The sun moves half
an inch. The journey will be
finished by tonight. Nothing
will matter in a million
years. I wonder if I gave
one frantic gesture it would
uncover all the complex
information, suddenly
silvery, riffling quickly
through the well-thumbed pages of

this ordinary place? Is
it a washroom in this case?
But here we are, and now. So
further instructions folded
in the wings are sure to seem
merely pernickety. I
know that if I blow on them,
they'll flicker open and be
right. Sunbeams stretch. Suspicions
glint. The questions narrow in
a more aggressive squint. This
is the arrangement on the
hot wall at midday. They stick
to it. What could I want that
they would give away? Rigid
with scorn, each cocks a minute
snook. However close I come
they won't exchange a look. They're
coded, rolled up thin, sealed with
a tweak, and then delivered
on the triangles of light
so accurately that you'd
swear that everyone had heard
a great voice speak. Jack staggers
between tables with the shock.
He leans so heavily on
a chair he makes it squeak. He
is tensed up and ready in
the gloom, no longer able
to confirm that this is the
reading room. In the silence
he gabbles explanations
in his head, spells words backwards
or counts syllables in lines
he could have said. He's aware
that I am mocking him, and
responds by taking trouble

with this idiot, the chair,
propping another silly
proof on four old puns in pairs.
Surely there must be something
that it's like to be a moth?
Some unique loveliness? To
believe in this would be as
if he creamed together runs
of interlacing ripples
being played on different
guitars. Transparent membranes
spread and glisten round his wrists.
His shoulderblades are braced as
he insists. Because he wants
a star, he rataplans his
drum, pressing it hard against
his abdomen. This could be
the best occasion for us
both to take a gamble on
the evening air. Jack nods.
I dry my hands. It is a
serious affair. We stare
at one another from a
distance, considering the
difficulties that are there.
We need to choose the roads and
hostelries. We must decide
exactly what the smell of
coffee is. Our picnic will
be nearer to the coast. The
food we have to share will be
scrupulously presented
on the grass, as a welcome
for any monster who might
pass. I expect a moth to
flutter round the tablecloth.

The Night Piece

The lock up is on. Someone
cackles in the goose house
at the policy of monsters.
In the white kitchen I
jump up and rub my hands.
Never a footprint out
there on the moonlit snow.
Then I squint. Then I know.
Plenty of small manifestos
wherever the blue mice go.

Mop and mow. Someone blows his
nose at the goose on duty.
I wade into the next gloomy
instalment, hissing through
my teeth, searching in straw
and strategy and all that
endless so and so. Then
the repartee runs briskly
round the rafters. I switch off
my torch and watch the eyes glow.

I must make a gate in case there's
a message. I make it twice.
The goose lies in wait, strict
with hate, in the barn. She
tots up her bill and the mice
shew two incisors each.
Certain truths cramp the corner
of the windowsill, but Jupiter
reflects on the pane. Or a
wandering lamp down the lane.

Try the outside tap, but
don't hold your breath.
The thick air has gone thin.
Listen to me. Little
is certain. A mouse springs
a trap. I massage bare skin as
goose pimples begin.
The narrower the gap
between curtains, the more
vivid the point of the pin.

Cronos collars the old yew
with iron. The darkest tree
sets out stars round its head.
The goose is the only Roman
left. She parades up and down
engrossed by the tip of her beak.
Why on earth should a sentry
seem so bereft? If I said
'Bo!' every dead inch of
the yard would squeak.

Exactly. The latch snaps. Now
the traveller could pass, but he's
pleased to lean on his cudgel.
Metal hugs the exhausted wood.
The port tastes of the vessel.
The bag stinks of cheese. The goose
stops, frozen, at the end of
her shadow. Stand and deliver.
The mice are delirious as they
wrestle in the crackling grass.